LE

GW00993568

A
Personal
Way of the Cross

ST PAULS

Cover and text images: Demetz art studio, Ortisei, Italy.
Used with permission.

ST PAULS Publishing
187 Battersea Bridge Road, London SW11 3AS, UK
www.stpauls.ie

ISBN 085439 637 3

Set by TuKan DTP, Fareham, Hampshire,UK
Printed by AGAM, Cuneo, Italy

ST PAULS is an activity of the priests and brothers
of the Society of St Paul who proclaim the Gospel
through the media of social communication

Introduction

Apart from the celebration of Holy Mass, there is no better meditative and contemplative prayer than the Way of the Cross. The Stations of the Cross are so important that the Church undertakes to do them every year during the Lenten season.

The graces and blessings received by meditating and contemplating each Station are so great that they are greater by far than any other prayer or act of worship. Such a powerful devotion, therefore, should not be left as an annual exercise for Lent alone, but should be embarked upon frequently throughout the year. Jesus once told Sr Faustina Kowalska, when he appeared to her, that the Sacrifice of the Mass was the greatest means of salvation for man; second to this was the meditation and contemplation of his passion and death on Calvary, by far the greatest source of benefit for the soul.

It is always good to say an act of sincere contrition before making the Way of the Cross.

An Act of Contrition

O Good Jesus, in your great mercy, have mercy on me. O most merciful Jesus, by that precious blood which you shed for sinners, I beseech you to wash away all my iniquities and to look graciously on me, a poor and unworthy sinner, as I call upon your holy name. Therefore, O Jesus, save me for your holy name's sake.

O Jesus, king of love, I trust in your merciful goodness.

For those who make the Way of the Cross, a plenary indulgence is granted under the usual conditions; that is:

Confession
Communion
One Our Father, Hail Mary and Glory be, for the Pope's intention.

You can make the Way of the Cross meditating on them in your homes, even while sitting on your bed.

Initial prayer

Say before the High Altar:

Almighty God, the magnitude of your love and mercy for us is so overwhelming that you sent your only Son Jesus to suffer and die on the Cross so that your people might be saved from the infernal fires. Through your Son's passion and death, awaken in us the reason for our existence here on earth, and your will as to how we should serve you in this world. Show us the pain sin causes you so that we may not grieve you by sinning again. In Your boundless mercy and love forgive all our transgressions, and pour down your blessings on this world so that we may not offend you again but live in complete obedience to your holy will.

Amen.

I

Jesus is sentenced to death

Jesus, in your boundless love and mercy do not abandon me. I adore you. It was the pride and wickedness of my humanity that demanded your crucifixion. I was there in my sin, and I now know how wicked and evil I was. In your boundless compassion, generosity and love, wash away all my offences. Let your graces and blessings dictate my thoughts, words and deeds so that I may glorify, praise and honour you always. Beloved Jesus, creator, redeemer, friend and brother, I love you beyond all words.

Holy Lord, through your love and mercy save me.

II

The Cross is laid on Jesus

Merciful Jesus, by your great love for us, you endured the thousands of insults, blows, spits and lacerations you were subjected to. Now you are forced to carry the Cross. Through this Cross of love and mercy deliver me from all my enemies, visible and invisible, and keep me always under your special protection so that I do only your Holy Will in order to gain eternal salvation.

Lord Jesus, let your mercy be my salvation.

III

Jesus falls
the first time

Holy redeemer, you are the Word that was, that is, and that shall always be. Through you all things were made and it is your power that sustains all on this planet. Yet I, together with the Jews of that time, condemned you in full knowledge of your innocence. At this first fall, O King of love, forgive me, for I trust in your merciful goodness. Grant that the Holy Spirit be my guide so that I may do only your will with love and joy in my heart as your devoted servant. Grant that I may never offend you again.

Beloved Jesus, may your love always be my guide.

IV

Jesus
meets his mother

Holy Mother, let me feel some of the pain that you endured at this meeting. Knowing how innocent your beloved Son Jesus was and unable to do anything about it, your tender heart was torn to pieces. What unimaginable pain you bore and how your heart must have bled. Pray for me, Holy Mother, for in my wretchedness I was the sword Simeon spoke of, that pierced your heart. Suffering Jesus, the anguish and pain that my wretchedness caused you and our Mother is unforgivable. Knowing better now, I come with a truly contrite heart to beg for mercy. Jesus, Son of Almighty God, look with pity upon me and through your mighty power and limitless mercy bring me to everlasting life.

Holy Mother of God, and my Mother too, pray for me a sinner, now and at the hour of my death.

Holy Jesus, wash me in your precious blood and I shall be whiter than snow.

V

Simon of Cyrene carries the Cross with Jesus

Jesus, Simon did not realise his privilege. I wish I had been there to carry the cross behind you, for you were burdened with all my sins. Your mercy and love for us is infinite, while your obedience to Our Father is absolute, so you carry not only my sins but those of the whole world from beginning to end.

O Jesus, through the memory of your suffering on the Cross, grant me the grace of a complete conversion, so that I may love you with my whole being, heart, soul, mind and body. It is you alone that I worship and adore, Lord.

Jesus meek and humble of heart, make my heart like yours.

VI

Veronica
wipes Jesus' face

Jesus, Lamb of God, the pain you absorbed from the beatings and the broken jaw and cheek bone you received racked your body with unbelievable pain. Your countenance was badly disfigured. It was marked and bruised, swollen and streaming with blood. Veronica, unable to endure it any longer, made bold and wiped your face. In your gratitude for that kindness and love, you left the image of your holy face on her towel. Give me the grace, sweet Jesus, to follow you with a sincere heart. May I always live in accordance with your holy will.

Imprint your holy face on my heart, mind and soul, so that I may never forget the reason for your passion and death and with a firm purpose of amendment I resolve never to offend you.

My Jesus, may my name be written in your heart.

VII

Jesus falls the second time

Adorable Jesus, you have fallen again and again; my sins tripped you up. The shouts of glee and screams of delight in the crowds each time you fell were those of my sins also. Jesus, I was wicked then and blind, and lived in darkness, but now, like Peter, through your grace I know and believe that you are Christ, the Son of God and the light of the world. You are the way, truth and life and so in you I place all my happiness and it is in you that I wish to live and die.

Beloved Jesus, grant that I may always live in you and for you.

VIII

The holy women weep for Jesus

Weakened by extreme pain and loss of blood, loving Jesus, the weight of your Cross has increased immeasurably in weight. You could scarcely stand, much less walk, and yet you were made to hurry with this load on your shoulder. Unrelenting, the soldiers dragged and hurried you up to the top of Calvary. The holy women who knew and loved you wept bitterly. In your compassion and love you consoled them saying: 'Weep not for me but weep for yourselves and for your children'. Yes, Jesus, we merit nothing but damnation. Holy God, creator, redeemer, brother and friend, save me for your holy name's sake.

Son of the Living God, you died for me, let me die for you.

IX

Jesus falls
the third time

My loving Jesus, you are the beginning and the
end of all things, full of life and virtue, and for
my sake you did carry this Cross. From the soles of
your feet to the crown of your head, there was not a
single spot on your body that was not in pain and
torment, now you have fallen for the third time.
Sadly, there were many such painful falls. By your
great torment and suffering, teach me to keep your
commandments through pure love for you. Give me
grace to receive with a worthy heart your precious
body and blood during my life, and especially at the
hour of my death.

My most holy Jesus, save me for your holy name's
sake.

X

Jesus is stripped of his clothes

My Jesus, now that you are on Calvary the soldiers eagerly rip the clothes off you; even the garments that stuck to your flesh. Looking at your bruises and the weakness of all your limbs, distended beyond belief we know that there could never be pain like yours.

Yet, uncomplaining and meek as a lamb, you surrender yourself to be crucified, and for love of me. There are no amends I can make that could in any way compensate for the wounds I caused you: wretch that I am. I throw myself at your feet, Lord, and beg forgiveness.

Jesus my saviour, I abandon myself to you now and forever.

XI

Jesus is nailed to the Cross

O Jesus, having shed your adorable blood so abundantly, you now submit humbly for the ultimate torture. Your tormentors, with indescribable cruelty, now stretch your body on the Cross, pulling you from all sides to nail your sacred hands and feet to it. O beloved Jesus, is there anything left for you to do for us that you have not done? Nailed to the cross you are raised aloft. The weight of your body on the nails caused you untold pain which penetrated to the very marrow of your bones.

Jesus, I know that I alone am responsible for all you suffered. All I have to offer is a promise of a perfect contrition, a firm purpose of amendment, and an absolute obedience to your commandments and holy will.

Tormented and tortured Jesus, through your pain and suffering convert me completely to be holy like yourself.

XII

Jesus dies on the Cross

Sweetest Jesus, in utter pain and abandonment you cry out: 'My God, my God, why have you forsaken me?'. Such pain and extreme anguish is more than I can bear. I weep to think of it. Dent my heart with the pain that you bore to help me think of you in every event of my life.

Forgetting your own torment and mortal agony you prayed for all your enemies saying: 'Father forgive them for they know not what they do'. For this prayer alone I thank you, Lord. Without it I would certainly be damned. Having accomplished our Father's wish, you now yield up your spirit. Late though it be, I throw myself before you and beg to be allowed to stay with you forever.

Immaculate Mother of God, please pray for me.

Jesus, remember me now that you are in your kingdom.

XIII

Jesus is taken down and placed in his Mother's arms

You were abandoned, my Jesus, by all your friends and relations. Only our sorrowing Mother and John remained with you enduring unimaginable pain and grief. Taken down from the Cross, you were placed in the arms of your Mother. Her untold sorrow rents her heart to shreds. Fill me with a remorse that I may never offend you again.

Mary, Queen of heaven and earth, pray for me for being the cause of the death of your beloved Son. Pray that I may be absolved from my sins against Almighty God.

Almighty and eternal God, spare this world and me for what we have done.

XIV

Jesus is laid in the sepulchre

Jesus, now you are finally buried. The world is all the poorer for having killed you. Those who did not believe in you thought that all was over. Then, three days later, there was consternation at the news that you had risen. There was joy not only in heaven, but also for all your followers, disciples and apostles here on earth. What unbelievable joy!

Loving Jesus, grant me the grace to resist the devil, the flesh and the world, that being dead to the world I will live for you alone. I beg you also to receive me, a penitent and an exile returning to you. Remember me, now that you are seated at the right hand of the Father.

Triumphant Jesus, may your kingdom come and your will be done on earth as it is in heaven.

XV

Jesus rises in glory

Conclusion

Say before the High Altar:

Jesus, you are Almighty God. Through your absolute obedience to the Father's will and your great love for all your brothers and sisters on earth, you have conquered sin and death by rising triumphantly from the dead. You have made it possible for all people to enter heaven. May praise and honour and glory and victory and power be to you, holy beloved Jesus in heaven and on earth now and forever and ever.

Jesus, by the shedding of your precious blood and by your glorious resurrection, graciously look upon me, a poor and unworthy sinner, as I call upon your holy name. Help me to obtain the forgiveness of the Father and help me to be good towards him. Help me, Jesus, to know what God gives me because sometimes I give up doing a good deed thinking it to be wrong. Holy and eternal God our Father, for the sake of your bounty and that of your son, who conquered sin and death for me, grant me forgiveness for all my transgressions. May praise and honour and glory and worship be to you, Almighty Father, in heaven and on earth, now and forever. I praise you, God.

Mary, Mother of my soul, I consecrate the last hours of my life to you. Come to me and receive my dying breath. When my life is ended, tell Jesus while presenting my soul to him, 'I loved him'. These words alone will secure the happiness of heaven and the joy of seeing you there for all eternity.

Amen.